The Exquisite Ordinary

by Rachel Whaley Doll

Special thanks to Lillie Whaley for taking the cover photo,
and for so many things!

This book is dedicated to all those that dare

to use the gifts they have been given.

Thanks for sharing.

Contents

One: Aware

Two: Grateful

Three: Inspired

Four: Fiction

Acknowledgments

I would like to acknowledge all those
that have spurred me on in my writing journey.
Especially to Patricia Sprinkle, David Maxwell,
Anna Marie McHargue and Phyllis Tickle
who have taught me so much
simply by talking with me about my work.
Your words continue to give me courage.

Part One:

Aware

Relax!

I bought new throw pillows. Somehow the bright blue chenille is like a whisper of spring promises on a gray February day. Not just the promise of warming weather, but the promise that if the mounds of snow and ice can give way to tulips and climbing roses waiting underneath - anything is possible in time.

I have always had trouble writing at home. Somehow, all the chores a house requires call to me as I try and relax to sit and write. I was struck recently with an epiphany of sorts.

Sitting in an airplane seat at the beginning of a long flight, I grew frustrated as I tried to fidget and wiggle into a comfortable position - it was *not* working. A quiet yet firm voice in my mind said, "You can't 'get comfortable,' you must learn to relax where you are."

Wow.

I figured if I could be completely relaxed lying on the floor after a yoga class, I could relax anywhere. I slowly began to visualize each part of my body relaxing and later stepped off the plane invigorated!

That realization spoke to the rest of my life, as well. Instead of spending years anxiously waiting, as if in line, for my heart's desires that may never be fulfilled; I will try to relax where I am today, and simply be in the present.

Just Start Swimming

I feel so grounded, and so lost. It would be easy to decide to get caught up in the day to day and let time slip by. I get so stressed and worked up, so anxious over the small things; packing lunches, cleaning the house, repacking the diaper bag, being on time *anywhere*!

But I'm too afraid to reach out and even touch the big things, doing something with my voice or putting my writing out there.

Why is it so much easier to stand frozen, letting the world push me numbly with the flow, never directing my own steps?

In the water, isn't it safer to swim in the direction of shore? Actually, no. If you find yourself too far out, it's safer to conserve your energy and go with the riptide, swimming parallel to the shore, until you feel the current lessen, hoping for rescue.

I don't want to let the current pull me slowly away from my destination and I *don't* need to be rescued. I'm not so far out that swimming for shore, choosing my own direction, would be too risky.

The earth will not shatter if I pursue my dreams. No one will go hungry, but dinner might be a little late sometimes! Unconsciously, I convinced myself that I need all the energy for the whole journey right now, instead of just enough to take the first steps.

There will be endless decisions that will need to be made along the way, but they will be millions of small ones, requiring only tiny shifts. The biggest one is definitely the first one, the decision to start.

Suddenly, the idea of reaching the end and realizing I simply went where the tide took me is no longer acceptable. It's going to be messy and maybe even painful at times.

I'm going to get it wrong more than once, and probably curse the day I started; but dammit, I'm going *that* way! I'm heading for *that* horizon, and I know I'm stubborn enough to get there.

The nice thing is, I don't know what to expect it will look like when I arrive. I just know I have gifts and stories and love to share, and they are doing nothing except weighing me down while I keep them snug and safe and tucked away.

Time to shed the fear and just start swimming!

A-Musing Meeting

I see a glimpse of my muse, shy and timid - or is that mischief in her eye? She's peeking around the corner, daring me to meet her eye. In my Busy-ness, I banished her months ago; or she stomped out in a rage at being ignored. I forget which now.

But we've missed one another more than we were mad, so I think we'll make up soon.

As children, the most offensive injustices were met with loud anger, brief silence (usually with wonderfully awful faces) and then an outstretched hand to move on to the joy of imagination shared. I miss that.

Today there usually is no loud cry over injustice, just a head shake and a feeling of helplessness. We don't stomp into the silence, rather we simply stop connecting; lulled into a zombie-like state brought on by laundry and dishes and our endless addiction to Stuff (buying, maintaining, accumulating, etc.) And then there is the ongoing affair with that abusive lover - the Light Up Box (read 'computer' or 'TV', whatever your lover's name is).

But every so often, a splash of sparkles in a stranger's dress, an unexpected twirl of melody, a glimmer of connection with a kindred spirit~ and the muse bounds back, wearing pink and orange and red together. Glorious in her beauty and undying love for me. Suddenly everything else falls away again, if only for a little while. . .

Oh to find the balance between writing and reality!

Rooted Together

A tree starts out by chance, almost casually. A seed is covered by enough soil, the rains come and life bursts forth. It's fragile at first, pushing with all its might towards the life giving light. So many things can end the saplings life; a footfall, too much rain, not enough, cold, heat. Yet if it survives, an intricate web of roots begins. Some roots shoot out and run into rocks. The root might be too weak and allow the rock to kill it. The root might be able to embrace the stone, making it stronger for the experience.

Either way, each root – short and weak or long and entangled, *each root* adds to the strength of the tree. Seasons effect it, slowing down its growth in winter, giving it time for reflection and rest. Spring and summer bring warmth and green leaves, new roots shoot out in all directions, drinking and growing stronger. Once the tree has matured, it flowers and maybe produces fruit.

That's how our relationship is, sweet spouse. We met by chance, casually getting to know one another. So many things could have ended the fragile sapling relationship; too much attention, not enough, different priorities or dreams, distance. Yet our relationship grew and roots shot out, our experiences together.

Sometimes we ran into rocks and that experience ended. Sometimes we embraced the hindrances, and it made us stronger. All our experiences, good *and* bad, weave our root system, making us stronger.

Seasons affect us, too. Winter brings lots of work for Aaron, the cold forces me indoors more often and makes time for reading, games, introspection; and depression if we're not careful.

But spring brings energy, lets us spend more time together outside, producing more root systems of shared experiences and lots of green leaves. We create so many things together; pottery, flowers, games. We're still waiting for the fruit to appear; yet we remain a healthy and growing tree, lovingly providing shade and limbs to climb on for those around us.

Screaming at God

This is a hard one, and a long time coming. I have not written much about our miscarriage, which happened many years ago, until now. I finally found the courage to relive a hard time, so that I could start to deal with it myself, and also reach out to others that have lived it.

There have been many people horrified to discover that I have had screaming matches with God. Not really matches, as I've only heard silence in return. But it was a safe kind of silence, when you know someone is there, strong and lovingly present.

People have said, "You're a southern belle, a minister's wife, for heaven sake, surely you have more faith than to scream at God!" I think that misses the point altogether.

I believe it's *because* I had faith that I screamed at God.

I think if we are honest, deep in the quiet places of who we are, most of us get mad at God at some point. I'm not sure what we think will happen if we say it out loud. I was always afraid to find out, until the miscarriage.

At the time, I was so broken and raw, I honestly didn't think about the consequences. It didn't matter what the rules of engagement were anymore. Life as I knew it was over. I didn't actually care what happened to me if I really told God what I thought. That afternoon, alone in my house, all I knew was that the tiny, growing being that had fought so hard to exist was now dead.

There had been weeks of doubling FSH levels (which it was supposed to do), and borderline levels, and blood draws every other day on the way to work. I would try all day to focus on the children I was educating, and take the phone call at 1:30 to let me know where my levels were that day. Usually there were children in my office, so I always wore a very straight poker face. We had spent three years trying to conceive, and we had finally done it. Almost there. The doctors said it could very well be that the child would live, and have severe birth defects. I found stories online saying perfectly healthy babies were born that started out this way. So many days I drove home bargaining out loud in the car with God. "We're almost there! I will love and care for this child, whatever happens. You can fix this! DO something!"

Then, one day it was over. December 18, 2003.

I stomped in the house slamming the door, throwing things. My two dogs stopped in their tracks, having been headed for our ritual afternoon reunion. They stayed close enough to watch me, but far enough away to show they were scared. I have no idea what I screamed that day, but everything I had been fighting to keep in balance came spilling out of my mouth. Eventually, my voice hoarse, I crumpled onto the floor in our bedroom. The dogs came in and sat on either side of me, leaning their bodies on mine in silent hugs. I wept in their fur until I fell asleep on the floor.

After that afternoon, I went through my days as a zombie. I showed up and did what was expected at work, church, and home. But my eyes were glazed and I felt nothing. Except guilt, I AM southern, there's always room for guilt! I remember feeling guilty for not being sad; guilty for not being there emotionally for my husband. But that was all. It was almost a relief to feel nothing for a change. My days were surrounded by creches, it was Christmas after all. There were many bitter thoughts about that single teenage girl; made pregnant by God. That's honestly how mad I was. Even Mary wasn't safe.

But as day bled into day, and I realized I wasn't struck by lightning, or squashed like a bug; it began to dawn on me that I might make it. I realized through that nightmare that God created me, just as I was. I was living honestly, saying what I felt to someone that loved me beyond measure; someone that loved me way more than I loved myself right then. I was safe with God, no matter how honest I was. There was such power in learning that I could be totally honest within myself and out loud with God.

Powerful, Silent Friend,

You continue to amaze me. When I am empty, when I am full of venom, when I am exhausted, you are there. Help me hang on when things are raw and outcomes are final and, oh, so painful. Let me feel your presence. Amen.

Power

My mind feels like the calm in the storm. Not because a storm is not raging. Not because I don't have strong feelings about the storm, and its possible consequences. Somehow, thankfully, I am calm in the midst of the storm simply because I can see far enough around me to know my anxiety will not affect the storm; it will only affect me.

I can tape the windows and store up water before, and clean up the debris afterward. I can hold a frightened animal and give comfort during the storm. But to fret about it assumes I have some measure of control over it, and to realize I cannot control the storm fills me with an entirely different feeling of power.

My sight has to extend beyond myself; I must take in the whole scene to realize my part. Realizing my part is small does not diminish my worth; a battery is a small part of an electronic device, but essential. While I know I am not the power source, and am glad I do not hold that responsibility; I do have a sincere responsibility to use and share the gifts I have been given; to stand up and do my part. I will not know how the ripples from my art will touch another, but having felt that touch from so many others, I have no doubt of its power. Power isn't something to gather and hoard and scheme to make larger. Rather, power is the energy that simply moves through us, giving and receiving it connects us to one another and to the whole.

Many times, when I have felt the power of God in my life, it is not in the still quiet moments I am alone with my Creator, although that happens occasionally. No, most often I experience the power of God through another person.

When someone else allows God's power and energy to flow through them, igniting the gifts placed in each vessel, I see a swirl and connection of beauty and power that could not happen without the willing vessel in quite the same way.

May you see and cherish your gifts, and allow God's power to move through you, igniting all of God's community.

The Night Before Sylvia

I uncovered an old journal, and found this letter to my youngest daughter, written the night before we met.

Tomorrow, finally, we will meet. I will look into your eyes and count your fingers and marvel at your nose. We will call a zillion people who wait with eager anticipation to learn about you. Daddy will hold you and his eyes will twinkle and he will fall in love with you; and I will, too.

Your sister is not quite sure what's going on, but she already knows she loves you and can't wait to tickle your toes. Family has travelled many miles to look into your eyes and tell you they love you on your very first day in the big wide world.

But for tonight you wiggle and move within me, trying to get comfortable; I think with very little success. You feel so huge and heavy inside me, your fingers seeming to find my hips, your feet and knees dancing on my ribs and lungs. And that bum! You are already quite the dancer, shaking your bum so often.

I am exhausted and sore and eager to meet you. I know tomorrow you will seem so light and small in my arms; and so beautiful and loved, cherished always and from the first moment, forever in my heart.

I love you, baby of mine.

Emerging Statement of Faith

For many of us, our faith is defined by assumptions, and never really examined in the light of day. Either out of a sense of fear of the unknown, or a sense of comfort that someone already spelled it out in black and white; we accept our beliefs without a second thought. Those assumptions have quietly caused callouses for years, never quite fitting right; but I was not sure what to do about it. Several realizations have presented themselves at once, and I feel it is time to begin putting them on paper.

I believe God created each person. Not to pass tests or complete a maze, but for the sheer joy of creating. I picture God mixing this gift with that passion and swirling in certain personality traits for zest.

Perhaps there is a messy palette strewn with colorful splotches, as God chews on a bit of bread and decides what to mix next. I believe people aren't created with a whole life plan in place, but with endless possibility.

This brings up God's Will. I do not believe that God draws out our experiences and puts us on a path. Rather, the things that we are good at are part of us so that we can connect with those around us.

I know I have felt nudgings to call this person, or help that person, and sometimes I take the time to listen and act. I am always glad I did, because there is joy in easing another traveller's journey.

I have also experienced times when someone helped me, out of the blue, because I had "been on their minds." I believe those times are someone listening to God.

But to say that God tests us, or chooses to make bad things happen, paints such a tedious and small picture of God to me. It feels like there is this spiritual energy in everything, some positive and some negative. We can choose to channel either one, and that has a powerful effect on our journey.

But when a child dies, or someone is murdered, saying that God did that to teach someone something, or for some other purpose lessens the worth of the one who died and seriously dements Gods image. I think that God sees such a bigger picture, the pain must be seen differently too. I believe this life is only part of what is, and probably a small part at that. I mean only to suggest a different perspective, not to belittle the pain in the world. It is real and should not be marginalized.

I believe Jesus was a real man. I believe he actively listened to God's nudging, and got it right way more often than most of us. I don't need to know which stories actually happened, and which were metaphors; it is not important in my understanding of who he was. If we, as Christians, simply studied the teachings of Christ, and tried to live as he taught; our churches and the world would be a much more peaceful place.

I think all the literal conversations only distract from the amazing truth in the stories found in the Bible. For instance, if the story of Jonah has to be literal, then my mind jumps to the smells present in a whale's belly, and how he was not injured, and the stomach acid. . .

The truth is in none of that. The truth of the story is that no matter where you are, or what trouble you're in, God is there.

You may still find yourself in the stomach contents of a whale, but you are not alone.

The truth of the story is that God needs you to use your gifts to share light with others.

The truth is that our hang ups and stereotypes of others only serve to get in the way of sharing the love of God.

This is definitely a work in progress, but I wanted to share where I was today. What an amazing journey faith is.

My Mother's Hands

I saw my mother's hand today. It was sticking out of my sweater, wiping home made cookie crumbs from my daughter's chair in my dining room. It made me incredibly homesick.

Instantly, I saw the design of black and white and gray that covered the kitchen floor of my childhood, and felt the hard wooden chair beneath me that I always sat in at the kitchen table. It made me want to grab a book and climb up in the Happy Chair, our La-Z-Boy rocker that was the place to go when Mom had a few minutes to read to me. Mom is hundreds of miles away, in our hometown.

But. . . the Happy Chair was re-covered (a mere 20 years ago) and now sits by my window, waiting for a book and a child and a grown up to fill it. Soon I will travel home for Christmas, bringing giggling children to my parent's home, to fill our days and hands with joy. Today, I will use these hands to give "one more cookie AGAIN please" to a sweet three year old. We will no doubt grab a book when the lunch dishes are done, and read in our Happy Chair.

I cannot wait to hold my mother's hands in mine again, and thank her for all those lazy days of my childhood; days that I am realizing were only lazy for me.

Three year old hands have cleared her dishes from the table and found a music box. They are holding ribbons as a beautiful dance unfolds in the living room.

Childhood is such a gift, not only to the child. I think those flutters in my chest are my muse and my childhood memories, holding hands and dancing with my daughter.

I Have Today

One morning, as I did research for a book proposal, I felt led to pray for some friends. I stopped and prayed, and the prayer grew longer. Then I heard myself add my book to the prayer, and felt a little voice respond "Not now. Put it aside and write what you know." Here's what I know today:

The beautiful green tree in my yard turned a brilliant yellow and lost most of its leaves while I wasn't paying attention. Usually, I love simply sitting with that tree as it stands in its golden glory, in the middle of autumn. The calendar and the house are too filled with things to be cleaned or completed these days. I cherish the people that surround me, but I'm noticing how often things and useless appointments are robbing me of precious connections.

I keep believing that somewhere there is a balance between cleaning and producing and experiencing joy. I think if I just organize better, or get rid of enough obligations or things, then I will step into a nirvana of balance and peace.

Perhaps simply acknowledging that both exist, I can begin to find peace in the midst of the the swirling leaves of the messiness of life and the peace of stopping to look.

I feel guilty to notice that Sylvie has been quite cranky and ill tempered lately. Some is, no doubt, due to the fact that she is three; and potty training is hitting a few bumps in the road. But perhaps part of her wilfulness and short tempered fits could be due to the fact that I am busier lately. Stopping to allow time for her pretending, together, is such a fleeting opportunity.

Already there are times she has no use for me, no desire to come to me for assurance or snuggles. Soon that will increase, and I will watch her learn to care for herself, needing me less and less.

I have been invited to become a mermaid, and play with her friend the butterfly, and I sometimes felt that the dishes or laundry or a million other things were more important.

After preschool, I hope to have some tea with a butterfly and a mermaid. Right now, I think I'll finish the dishes so they don't steal my attention later. Thankfully, I have today. And the realization that it can be filled with so much more.

Longing for Montreat

For some of us, there is a place that so resonates with our very souls, that no matter how many miles or years separate us from that place, we feel as connected to it as if it were just down the street.

For me, Montreat Conference Center, in the mountains of North Carolina, has been that place for most of my life. Whether attending conferences, working in various capacities, or just stopping through while vacationing, Montreat is a beautiful and deeply spiritual place.

While riding in the car the other day, a memory so filled my thoughts, that I scrounged around and found the back of a coloring book so I could write the following love letter to Montreat.

Montreat – an amazing potter's wheel. No matter your age, no matter how many times you feel you have been fired in the kiln, driving through those Montreat Gates is like climbing on the potter's wheel that is Montreat. You are once again wet clay, open to the gentle molding of our ever present Creator.

Somehow it's easier to listen in Montreat, to the quiet voice of God and believe the things you hear; to let down your guard and let God mold what will become in your life.

The others that come to Montreat see you as a child of God, and act as the hands and feet of Christ, working together to learn and create and grow.

Then, with full hearts and friendships that weave connections far and wide, it's time to leave Montreat, but only for a while. You will be back, for a piece of your soul will always be there.

Inhaling Bedtime

It is late as I climb the stairs for bed. I am not finished with the day's chores, and it weighs on me; but the day is done.

I open the door to Robyn's room and inhale the peacefully invigorating scent of menthol, and the sound of silence. Tonight she is healthy and sleeping soundly.

Silently I move into Sylvia's room. There she lies, in the same position she said, "In Jesus name we pray, Amen," so many hours ago at bedtime. Her hair smells of baby shampoo, so much that my breasts ache to nurse her. My milk is gone, she is weaned, aches of sweet memory.

Down the hall in my own room, I pull back the sheets, set the alarm and inhale the musky, manly scent that is Aaron; my lips linger on his arm as he sleeps, his quiet breath so even and smooth.

All the scents and sounds of peaceful happiness swirl together in my soul, sweeping out the clutter in my head, gently untangling the knot in my stomach.

The whole of me relaxes into this beautiful life; this glorious time of renewing sleep that awaits. Sometimes in hindsight, I see the beauty of what I had; but I cannot recall feeling this completely whole in the moment.

What a gift.

Spirit is Moving

I could feel no wind on my face, just the warmth of the early summer sun. Yet the huge, old tree just beyond the playground fence danced and swayed in the breeze. I found it comforting.

I am talking to Spirit a lot these days, and listening. I am following the quiet urgings she whispers, most of which lie just outside my comfort zone. I trust the winds of change that I see working in others, and I'm beginning to feel her breath on my cheek as well.

Slowly, ever so slowly, I am beginning to trust the gifts I know I have held all my life. Until now, I have only had the courage to unwrap them once in a while, share them with those closest to me, and quickly wrap them up again. I'm starting to forget why I needed to keep them so protected; starting to enjoy the feeling of the warm sun on their faces. I think it's because now, I only want them to be what they were created to be.

For years I glanced at my gifts, and then stared at the works of masters, professionals, other people's gifts obviously "better" than mine. I packed mine away in shame.

The gifts are growing restless. They do not desire to win awards, or compete or be held up to any standard. They are simply asking to be held in the light. They are from Spirit, from my Creator, and they deserve to be cherished and fed and, yes, held in the Light.

I think I'll recycle their boxes, they won't be needed any longer.

Robyn's "Rememberings"

My oldest daughter is three and a half and I covet her ability to remember everything she hears. This morning, I am standing at the kitchen sink, doing dishes after breakfast while she finishes up. She's telling me about her most recent visit with a particular 'pretend friend.' Thankfully, today I was paying attention.

I ask, "Whatever happened to your pretend friends that were colors? I haven't heard you play with them lately." Robyn nonchalantly replies, "Oh they died."
"Oh no!" I quickly respond, "I'm so sorry!"
"It's okay, I'm not sad anymore," she says, as she concentrates on trying to build something with apple slices.

"How is it possibly okay?" I ask.

Her little hand covered her chest and she replied, "I'm not sad because I can remember them right here whenever I want. My Grandma told me that. Don't you remember?"

And yes, a couple of months ago we watched a video about Babar, whose mother died. We were trying to explain to Robyn what that meant. I told her that all the parts of a person that love and think, those parts go to Heaven to be with God and all the other people that have died; and you just don't need the other parts anymore. Grandma and Grandpa were visiting. Robyn looked up at Grandma with wet eyes and said, "Grandma, I would be so sad if you died. Don't do that, okay?"

I cannot imagine how hard it was for my mother-in-law to look into those pleading brown eyes full of concern and not melt, but she smiled and gently talked to my daughter about death. She pressed her hand to Robyn's chest and told her not to be sad for too long, because all the love they shared and all the 'rememberings' of things they had done together were right there, in her heart.

"It's all in there for you to keep," her wise Grandma said. "Forever and ever?" asked Robyn. "Forever and ever," Grandma replied.

This entire conversation was retold to me at the breakfast table, two months later, while she played with pancake parts and smeared syrup in a pattern on the table. Maybe it's not such a big deal that she doesn't remember to put her coat in the closet or pick up all the blocks; she's got important stuff in that little head, and more gets added every day.

Finally Spring

There's still a chill in the air, and a need for the wind chill to be listed on the daily weather report, but everyday Robyn finds another sign that the season is changing. "Look Mommy, purple flowers! What's that big black hill? It wasn't there before!" The mountains of pure white snow are giving way, slowly, to mounds of ugly gray and black crud; the result of months of pushing snow and ice and dirt away from parking spaces, and it couldn't be more beautiful. Ditches are full, the canal has yet to be filled, but creeks and rivers, ponds and even yards are swollen with the winter's wet and bountiful left overs.

The boisterous honking overhead that felt hopeless amid colorful leaves not so long ago, is now teeming with excitement as snow birds announce their return. The ducks 'wrestle' in the middle of the pond and search for nesting spots while children learn new tricks on the playground equipment. Their bodies have grown and strengthened in their snow suits and it's fun to see them try out their new wings.

I have never been a gardener, but lately my fingers itch to dig into the earth, to plant the whispers of life and wait to watch them grow into plants and burst forth with fruit and color. I remember past springs when I was so jealous of the earth and its new life.

As we struggled with infertility, I felt left behind and wondered what was wrong with me. But today, sleep deprived by the screams of a hungry little one, I can't help but grin, and wipe away a tear, for the beauty and abundance that is shivering to life all around me.

Creator of All, help me remain caught up in this joy, celebrating the simple miracles that surround me, no matter the season.

Experiencing with ALL the Senses

The taste ~ of a sun warmed strawberry, so ripe you
    know it's sweetness will run down your chin.

The feel ~ of the warm ground in late afternoon,
    whether barefoot at the beach, with a slight breeze
    when the sand is cool on top and warm deep down;
    or with your hands in the garden, when you can
    actually FEEL the life in the soil.

The smell ~ of bread so fresh you have to close your eyes to breathe it in.

The sight ~ of your very own driveway after a long drive, when you know you will finally be in your own bed soon.

The sound ~ when the TV's been on too late at night, and you didn't realize how loud it was until you turned it off; that amazing silence envelopes you and a sigh escapes.

God really is everywhere, in all that we encounter, whether we are paying attention or not.

At bedtime tonight, Robyn wanted to sing a new prayer to God. She started singing the "Itsy Bitsy Spider" and I said, "Hey, I thought you were going to pray!" She said, quite earnestly, "But I AM praying, Mom! You said I can tell God anything, and so I'm teaching God my favorite song. You can learn it too if you want."

Wow. How often do I forget that I *can* tell God anything? After she finished the song, she told God about the new purple flowers coming up since the snow went away, and about Blue, her pretend friend, and his birthday party . She ended by saying, "I love you God, Amen."

Dear God, today let me taste you, and see you in the mundane, amazing life that surrounds me. May I feel the freedom of a child to share everything with you, and to hear you whisper, to smell your creation, to feel your presence. I love you, God. Amen.

Family Cards

Mother's Day

No matter how many miles separate our bodies; our souls are forever interlocked, woven together by strands of late night conversations, shared secrets, recipes, dreams, tears and (of course) bubbles.

I am reminded every day of the many ways I have been blessed by being your daughter; and I am the woman I am still becoming because of the strength, love and lessons I have learned and still learn from you.

I thank God everyday for the gift of you, but especially today. Happy Mothers Day to a beautiful teacher, friend, mother and woman.

Anniversary

True love

   learns to be stubborn *and* flexible,

   strong *and* gentle,

   quiet when needed, and bold in other times.

Through years of experiences, both good and bad,

   your love story has shown many

   the blessings of beautiful, imperfect, amazing love.

We are so blessed to be part of your journey.

   Even though I forgot the day,

I remember with joy all you have taught us

    through love, through example, through prayer.

Happy Anniversary, Mom and Dad,

    may your love ever deepen

    as together you share this amazing journey.

Arboretum Oasis

In the afterglow of the holidays, we went to visit Aunt Lois in Buffalo. The morning after a wonderful visit with the cousins, we decided to go to the Arboretum just a couple of miles away, or so I thought. From the moment we stepped inside, it was a world away.

The silence seemed to even absorb the noise of three year old excitement, or perhaps she was in awe as well. We went from room to room, seeming to go deeper and deeper into peacefulness.

At one point, Robyn found a bench hidden away. We had traveled over a wooden bridge, spent time watching the enormous goldfish, in their yellows, whites and orange hues gracefully traversing the same waters, over and over.

I swear this is where someone thought of the screen saver. Over the bridge and up half a flight of wooden stairs, there was a bench, all alone. Sitting on it, you could see down through the plants to a waterfall crashing behind some trees.

The warmth and silence were broken only by the pounding of the falls, and it looked like a painting to see snow and piercing wind beyond the wall of windows.

Robyn decided the game of the moment would be to tickle Mommy and then run down the stairs and over the bridge to tickle Daddy, who was sitting on another bench with Aunt Lois and the stroller containing a babbling Sylvie. (I should mention, we were virtually alone in the Arboretum!)

What a wonderful game! My job was to sit and wait for her to come back. Listening to the waterfall in that balmy warmth was a long overdue massage for my soul. I tickled the appropriate child when she giggled past, and sat long after the game was over soaking in the smells and sounds. What an oasis!

The experience gently nudged my muse awake once more. Hopefully I will cherish my muse enough to give her space, whether the Christmas tree is still up in February or the laundry pile grows taller than my husband. She deserves at least as much time as dinner! Later, I cherish the memory by writing; I forgot how nourishing it is to feel the keys under my fingers and know my thoughts and feelings are swirling and spilling out. If only I enjoyed exercising my body this much!

Part Two:

Grateful

Sewing on the Porch

The tireless little two year old body finally gave in to the sleep that stalked it for over an hour. Her ringlets hit the light one last time as I dim the room and sneak out. Some nights I really am living the fairy tale. But on the way down the stairs, the list is breathing down my back. So many little and inconsequential things that have to be done. Tonight.

Everything is touched by the moist air that just won't cool off, no matter how hard that motor runs in the window unit. One of the things on my list is replacing the buttons on a dress handed down to Robyn, one she will wear to church tomorrow. I grab the dress and my sewing basket and head out to the screened in front porch, the coolest room in the house.

A quiet breeze instantly soothes my anxiety as I collapse into the rocker. I sit and sew by the light of the dining room window, and feel suddenly as if I am not alone. It's not the feeling that someone is on the sidewalk, that's a different feeling altogether. This is a powerful, peaceful feeling of connection, realizing how many women in my family have sat here over the years. Not on this porch, of course, but I can physically feel the connection to so many aunts and grands sitting in their rockers mending a hand me down, making sure everything is ready for Sunday services.

I am calm in a way I have seldom experienced. For a while after the mending is done, I sit on the porch, breathing in the contented sighs of all the women in my family.

She's long since outgrown that dress, but I can't seem to get rid of it; after all, it's an heirloom now.

Apples and Fruitfulness

Today I walked into my kitchen with my half share of fruits and vegetables, a weekly abundance of flavor and nutrition from Kirby's Farm Market, our local CSA (Community Supported Agriculture). Each week, I am excited to find a new food to try, or a recipe to energize my relationship with a food I've known all my life.

This week, early autumn, there was a large bag of apples. No surprise, but by gently washing them and placing them in my cobalt glass bowl, they became art. I simply sat and looked at them.

The colors were amazing, so many hues of red and yellow stretching out to cover the flesh beneath. Golden greens without a single color variation, even amid the fluctuations of weather we've had. The smell was clean and soothing, rich and simple at once.

I admit I couldn't resist, and crunched in to one of the red and yellow orbs. In the silence of the house, the noise was surprising! The juice that flowed down my chin was a delight.

A friends' daughter collects the apple seeds whenever anyone opens an apple in her presence, and after they are dried she adds them to her collection. That container of apple seeds is carried around reverently, and she loves to describe the process from seed to tree to apple. She's never planted one, or even asked to as far as I know, but the promise of abundance in that little container is very real to her. I smile as I reach the core, and spread out the seeds to dry for her.

I am struck as I see all of us as that little container; how much promise we hold, and so often keep it shut up within us. Passions that we see as hobbies, to dabble in when we finish our responsibilities. Duties we perform without ever realizing what a struggle those duties are for others.

Every day, we choose what to do with all the parts of who we are, whether we realize it or not. Going through the motions of our day, our calendar, we often let opportunities to connect get lost in the punctuality of our culture. We think, 'wouldn't it be nice if I could. . .' and then the light turns green and off we go, to the next item on our agenda.

The nourishment and enjoyment of experiences we could share are kept safe inside our souls; will they eventually rot from disuse like this apple? If the seeds of what could be are simply tossed in the garbage without a thought, how many others will not know the joy of an apple, how many trees will never be?

It can be overwhelming to think of all we leave undone. But by slowly realizing the choices we are making, we can bring joy and fulfillment to ourselves and so many others.

Unwrapping our Dreams

Yes, there is probably someone else that can do that thing you do better than you.

But chances are, they are not standing where you are. You are surrounded by people, right now, that would love to hear and see and share in that gift you have that you are hesitant to share. I believe if everyone shared with abandon, the gifts and talents they hold, dreams everywhere could be realized.

The secret is - together we hold the pieces to one another's dreams.

What if we opened our gifts together, like a great big Christmas morning, wrapping paper and pretty bows thrown with abandon; and then we *really* looked at everyone's gifts and how we might use them together.

Oh, what magic we possess! When we get over ourselves enough to reach out and share the gifts we hold, the pieces of other people's dreams- we leave room for someone to help us realize our own dreams. Nothing lost, only joy to be gained.

When we share our gifts we can begin to achieve the dreams of all of us.

So dream on!

An Aunt's Love

My Grandmother's sister had nice things, but her things were never the focus of her life. The tall majestic china cabinet that stood in her dining nook was so smooth to the touch. Dark wood made sloping proud lines in the glass doors. And in the long center drawer, nestled in the napkins on the far right, there were always chocolates to discover. The mahogany rocker in the sitting room sang a beautiful melody as I rocked in it. I remember the cool smooth feeling of the wood against my fingers as I rubbed the arm of it, or the end table in the living room.

She had a smile that beckoned you into a hug, and she smelled of lilac or some other faint flowery scent. There was always fresh pimento cheese, homemade in Mason jars, in the refrigerator. I never liked celery as a child, but would slather her pimento cheese on it as a treat at her house. The smell of her roast cooking was true magic!

I think each grandchild and cousin felt they were her secret favorite. Each of us felt welcome to stop by for a visit, whenever. How I wish I had more often. I can still close my eyes and feel her skin; wrinkled, soft, cool. She would gently hold my face between her hands, as if holding a cherished gift; or put my hand in between hers and squeeze.

Her eyes held so many colors in them, and twinkled and danced when she smiled. Somehow, she was as productive as her sisters; keeping a clean home, creating in the kitchen, always looking nice. But I can't remember seeing her fret. There was a peace to her, a joy in her eyes like a hidden treasure.

No matter how long she lived, I would still wish for one more visit; to hear the screen door whistle as I burst through.

I long to see her dry her hands, drop what she was doing and watch her eyes twinkle, her whole face smiling with joy at *me*; to feel her small, bent body envelope me in an encompassing hug that filled my soul. The strength in the spirit of that frail body was pure and abundant.

It is no surprise that her heart kept going after the rest of her body stopped. Even after she stopped communicating, she did not rest until my mother and I assured her we would take care of her sisters. The doctors said they did not know why her heart kept going, so long after the rest of her had shut down.

I know. The strong pure love that filled that heart surrounds us still.

Stain Glass

There is a song by Diana Jones called "Cracked and Broken"(from the album "Better Times Will Come") that has me mesmerized. One line is "Cracked and broken and beautiful, that's how the light shines through." That line has ridden many miles in my head, and brought so much to a light of its own.

In a piece of stain glass art, each tiny piece of glass has a story; has been on a journey that includes beauty, pain, creativity, loss. Each piece comes together, deliberately placed by an artist into a thing of beauty. Alone, the glass shard is just a dangerously sharp sliver of color.

But once safely nestled in the strong mortar, surrounded by other shards, we are all safe, our sharp edges covered and surrounded so that, through the safety of the artist's mortar, we can create with others a thing of beauty.

Art through which our Creator's light can shine onto the faces of *all* God's children.

Leaf Dancers

The sound of applause filled the fall air, as the wind blew through the tops of the trees. As if on cue, a troupe of dancers clad in gold, orange and red pirouetted across the cloud covered stage.

Giggles and anticipation filled the air as a young voice yelled at the top of her healthy lungs, "Ready, set, GO!" and then flew down the hill and disappeared into a large pile of leaves and joyous squeals.

The trees continue to drop their dancers out of the sky, the wind continues to carry them across the stage.

As for us, the darkening sky draws out yawns from tiny mouths; bedtime beckons. More leaf pile adventures will have to wait until tomorrow's dawn.

First Snow

Even the forecast of snow

is exciting this year, with a four year old.

And in the morning, long before I should be awake

a tiny nose touches mine.

"It snowed *everywhere*!" she whispers.

Together we float downstairs and open all the shades.

We stand together silently, drinking in the scene.

Minutes tick by. Finally she moves.

Suddenly we are outside;

she falls into the snow,

boots, nightgown,

huge snow angel grin.

It has begun.

(Originally published in 'Motherly Musings: Thirty Women and Men
Reflect on the Roller Coaster Ride that is Motherhood,' available in paperback
at http://www.unlimitedpublishing.com/wells in the US, UK and EU.)

Crayons

We use our energy and our crayons to draw lines around

things; what is ours, what is not.

Who is ours, who is not part of us.

We waste our crayons.

Always marking territory

    instead of drawing connections and creating beauty.

Draw what dances in your soul,

    what will meet the needs of those without crayons,

and the world will be filled

with a colorful and beautiful peace.

If you have the courage,

    extend your hand and share your crayons.

What happens next could reshape the world.

Growing Joy

Tiny toes balance the body that will not be stilled.

Her mind ever racing, connecting, exclaiming.

The kaleidoscope of emotions plays across her face

    with no filter, completely pure.

Every day brings to me varying amounts

    of exhaustion, anxiety, pressure;

But to her each day is a new exciting exploration,

    no rushing, only experiencing.

I can get caught up in the pressure, or in glimpses

    of the beautiful personality being created

    in that ever growing mesh of nature and nurture.

The anxieties in my life, whatever they are,

  are no bigger than I allow them to be.

It's not about stopping the world to be with my child,

  it's about traveling the journey together, and

  watching the road as often as I watch

  her experience it.

And now I have to go, there is a beautiful song

  being sung in the next room,

  and the puppet show is about to start!

Soaking It In

Tomorrow there will be time for thank you notes and church nursery schedules, for laundry and meals for those in need. Tonight there is no guilt in putting my feet up and pulling out the notebook. Or for sipping my second cup of schnapps laced coffee. So many messy details threaten to wind tentacles around this fragile peace.

But the peace is gaining strength.

I checked on the girls a few minutes ago. Not because I thought anything was wrong, I just wanted to look at them. There is no whine, no joy, no need written on their faces. There is no discovery or anger, just the utter beauty of a child. Perfectly formed lips open just enough to glimpse a tooth or two. Fingers wound around something soft and reassuring.

There are still tears if wonder on my cheeks when all is quiet and the dim lights soften the edges of all that is out of place. The misplaced tiara whispers of a grand adventure, and the days clothes crumpled on the floor show signs of dessert.

I don't think it's rose colored lenses I see my life through. Rather it is the clarity that comes from living without, from watching life slip away too soon, from realizing a hard won dream.

Today my life is beautiful, and I will take the time to simply soak it in. May you enjoy the sights of the beauty that surrounds you.

(Originally published in 'Motherly Musings: Thirty Women and Men Reflect on the Roller Coaster Ride that is Motherhood,' available in paperback at http://www.unlimitedpublishing.com/wells in the US, UK and EU.)

Crazy Beautiful Bedtime

There was lots of running, giggling, jumping and hiding in the closet together as Daddy moved Sylvie's bed into Robyn's room, so Uncle Bill will have a room while he visits.
"This is going to be a real alive sleepover, Sylvie! Just you and me!" Robyn whispered across the room.

Long after Robyn fell asleep, finally, I heard Dora's voice, from Robyn's toy, as Sylvie investigated the room free from the watchful eye of, well, anyone. I finally went in and we cuddled a few minutes, until she said "Okay, Mommy, all done."

With that, she rolled over and closed her eyes. I just had to stop and record this tiny stitch in the amazing tapestry that is being woven so quickly.

First Night at Stony Point

Earlier tonight, we sat around a campfire getting to know missionaries back from far away places, young adult interns and volunteers that were Christian, Jewish, or Muslim. They were all adults of various ages and stages of life, volunteering their time and talents at Stony Point Center. This beautiful conference center of the Presbyterian Church, USA, is located by the Hudson River near New York City. It is also the home of the Community of Living Traditions, a multifaith residential community dedicated to building residential community, engaging faith, and cultivating nonviolence.

The fireflies blinked big beautiful light as laughter rang out, and s'mores were created and devoured. Sylvie got the first s'more of the night, and of her life, and held it for over an hour, gently licking it and taking tiny bites, until it was taken away at bedtime and replaced with wails of heartbreak.

We heard stories of many journeys, and learned how their faith traditions shaped who these people had become, and were becoming. All of us had a deep faith in God, and a deep commitment to justice for all people. Robyn and Sylvie and a new friend ran and played and giggled, finding rocks and, later, snuggling close to parents as the moon rose.

But they also listened. Robyn and Sylvie sat motionless, with wide eyes, as a new Jewish friend told stories, complete with great sound effects.

Sylvie brought clover flowers to strangers around the fire, to a tall blonde Christian college student, and an African American Muslim woman in a beautiful blue and green head scarf. She looked up at them with wide, happy eyes.

I asked Robyn earlier today what she thought of Stony Point so far. She said she liked it, and there were lots of new people. Robyn is not terribly outgoing at first, so lots of new people wasn't necessarily a good thing. I told her that the people she was meeting here with Mommy and Daddy were safe people, like at our church at home, she could talk to them. I said even though they are lots of different sizes and ages, they were like our church family while we were here.

"Their skin is lots of different colors, too. I like that," Robyn replied. I like that, too. I cherish the journey we will have here, the images, memories and friendships we will come away with. I look forward to the questions that will flow out of these experiences, both from me and from my children.

What an amazing gift to watch my children learn and befriend and teach. Oh, help me focus on the joy of new discoveries as they wander so far from their schedule!

Tidbits

One in galoshes, the other in plastic dress up shoes, both in pajamas. They are running around our yard playing tag at bedtime. There is magic in the cricket's summer song.

Sylvia can only say "Potty words" (poop, toilet, etc.) in the bathroom. Some days she runs in there, not to potty but to stand there giggling saying "toilet, **toilet**, *TOILET!*" Words are so powerful.

Today there are glitter and feathers, dog hair and beach sand in the dust pan. Every mop day, without fail, the dining room chairs I move into the study are lined up to become a bus or a carriage or some other magical place. Thank you, God, for the fairy princesses in my life, and the adventures we have together.

Conversation about the Cemetery

As we were driving home from a visit to Papa's office, we passed the cemetery where my grandmother and lots of our family are buried. "Do you know what that is, Robyn?" my mother asked.

"Oh, that looks like a cemetery. I've been to lots of them with Daddy on walks and when we are geo-caching. There's lots of pretty flowers there, and big stones with names and numbers on them."

"In that cemetery, Grandma Atha is buried." I told her.

"What's buried?" came the quick reply.

Um, a moment to think. . . "When someone dies, all the parts that love, all the parts that think, and all the parts that remember, those parts go to Heaven with God. All the other parts aren't needed anymore, and we bury them in the ground, with the person's name on a stone above the ground, so we have a special place to go and think about that person."

After another moment of silence, she replied, "But we can think of that person anywhere! All the good parts are in heaven anyway. I guess it's good that all the rest of the parts are together, at least, with parts of other people from their family."

Tomorrow we might even pull in and walk around. . . I think that was enough for one day.

Robyn and God

Sometimes Robyn has lots of questions about God, all at once. Tonight's was, "Does God have a belly?"

"I don't know," I answered, "What do you think?"

"I think God has a really big belly, where all the babies live until they go into a mommies' belly. All the babies in this world and all the other worlds. That's a lot of belly!" She giggles and juts out her belly.

"Wow. And even though God is so big, and does so much, God knows you, Robyn, and loves you very much."

"God loves you, too, Mommy. You don't say that as much, I think you forget."

Wow. She sees a lot for a little one. Things are quiet for a moment. . .

"Mommy, what does God's voice sound like?"

"I think it's kind of like a whisper in your head; not like a boy or a girl voice, just a whisper," I reply.

"Sometimes, can God use a person's voice?" Robyn asked in a whisper.

"Yes" I say with tears in my eyes, "God uses all our voices, when we let it happen."

Mirror Image

I stood naked, looking in the mirror. It was just after my second child's first birthday, and she had just been weaned. Years of hormones from fertility drugs, three pregnancies and two births had left me with a body I didn't recognize. I remembered arms that didn't hang funny. There had always been a little blip of extra around my waist, but I now looked like I might be expecting again. I wasn't.

As I stood there taking stock of all these things, my three year old silently slipped into my room. I startled as a little voice asked, "Who are you mad at, Mommy? Your face looks angry." Thankfully, it was one of those rare moments when I saw clearly the bigger picture, and said something that would change both of us.

I slipped on my dress and pulled her into my lap as I sat down on the bed. "I'm not mad, honey. I was looking at the ways my body has changed lately."

"Yeah," she said, as she stroked my arm, "It's kind of lumpy in places. Is that bad?"

I smiled and hugged her, and from a sacred place the words I needed came to be shared with her.

"When Sylvia was growing in my body, I needed lots of energy to keep her safe and help her grow, until she was big enough to come out. My body also stored up energy so I could feed Sylvia after she was born. It takes a lot of energy for a woman's body to make milk. So my body stored up all the energy it could to get ready for all these things. Your body stores energy as fat, so you can carry it around with you and have it whenever you need it.

Now I'm all done growing Sylvia and feeding her from my body, and there is still extra energy stored in lots of places. But if I exercise my body, it will use the extra energy and get rid of it."

She snuggled me silently for a few minutes and then jumped down to go play. I decided that day, for my child, to never berate my body in front of her. It had been through some pretty amazing things and, God willing, would carry me through many more adventures. I didn't want my hang ups to color her body image.

Then a most beautiful thing happened. I consciously stopped making those degrading comments under my breath about my body.

Later, I realized I had stopped feeling guilty about the skinny clothes I couldn't wear in my closet. I moved them out of sight, so all the clothes I *could* see fit nicely. What a difference it made as I started my day! Little by little, beginning in that tiny moment looking into those trusting brown eyes of my daughter, I began to cherish myself.

This body is not perfect, but it is mine, and I am a beautiful person. My daughters see and notice that different people have different shapes. But they never hear their parents comment that someone is "fat" or "skinny." We notice someone's smile, or beautiful eyes. Sylvia loves to compliment ladies on their shoes and earrings.

I know when hormones begin to invade their bodies, we'll have lots more conversations about body image, and I hope for clarity on those days, too. So far, it looks like we're all doing all right.

Part Three:

Inspired

Journey with Lynda Barry

I embarked on a beautiful, creative journey by reading Lynda Barry's 'What It Is' (Drawn and Quarterly, 2008, available at amazon.com). Lynda draws, paints, writes, cuts and glues to express the magical jumble of creative thoughts that fill her mind. She is at once tormented and comforted by ideas and memories. I relate quite well. It is refreshing to see illustrations that are not necessarily 'pretty' or 'right' but instead dig deeper into the meat of the concept she is discussing, and into the reader's own head.

My friend, Christine Green, and I decided to journey through Lynda's book together, sort of. We both blog, and decided to blog as we read, and created.

This section, "Inspired," is filled with discoveries from that journey, as well as writings that came from exercises she suggests in the book. Christine's beautiful insights can be found at grownupsarelikethat.blogspot.com .

In the book, Lynda Barry asks "Why is there anxiety about a past we cannot change? The top of my mind has no answer for this." (Barry, pg. 6) And yet she is constantly thinking of things she wished she hadn't said or had done differently. I live there, too! I'm not sure how I think these worries will change today or tomorrow, but perhaps it will at least make me think more often *before* I speak. Sometimes that filter in my head is too clogged to work properly. I wonder how you clean that filter.

WOW.

What if writing and drawing and art could be a way of getting all those juicy morsels out of our heads that we can't say in polite conversation?! Lynda goes on to say, "I believe they are the soul's immune system and transit system." (Barry, pg. 17) That's so true! She suggested we write down a story that "you think cannot be true." (Barry, pg. 19).

Papa's Eyes

The story actually happened, but never seemed quite real. When I was thirteen, my grandfather had a brain aneurysm and died suddenly. We had seen him only a few days before, and he was fine. I remember being so angry. I could not imagine why my father would tell such a lie about his dad.

But on my thirteenth birthday I was given a hug and a card with twenty bucks in it, and then we rode the hour's drive to go to a funeral. Usually, there was a cake and a party and friends over for my birthday. That year, those things didn't matter. I remember needing to see Papa at the funeral to realize Dad wasn't lying. It was so final.

Then, about a month later, we visited my uncle, Dad's brother. He sat all the kids on the floor and read us a letter. In the letter we learned Papa's eyes had been donated to a nine year old girl who had been blind since birth, and now she could see. At the time, I had no idea you could even do that. I remember being sad that he was buried without whatever part they needed, but proud that he had asked that his eyes be used by someone else.

I spent weeks thinking how this tree or that kid would look to this girl that was using Papa's eyes. Things didn't seem quite so final. It was comforting to know his eyes were somewhere close by, delving into books or crinkled with laughter.

While the rest of him no doubt continues to look down on me, willing me to eat ice cream for dinner straight from the box; it is wonderful to know his eyes are living a rich and amazing life of their own.

Love you, Papa.

The Two Questions

Today, I am reading what Lynda writes about creating, about how and why we go about it.

"But the two questions find everybody. 'Is this good?' 'Does this suck?'... For the next 30 years I chased after only good drawing. While I drew, my main feelings were doubt and worry, and when I finished my only feelings were relief and regret. I never drew for fun any more - and I'd forgotten about that strange floating feeling making lines on paper used to give me. I'd forgotten how stories used to bubble up out of the lines and surprise me. It is why I started drawing – to meet those lines and stories." (Barry, pg. 123)

There have been days when I had to pull over and scrounge around under the car seat to find a stub of pencil or a pen, and write on an old receipt, or on the bottom of a tissue box. Sometimes the stories or ideas in my head get so big and loud, all I *can* do is stop and let it out.

Sometimes the story is falling out so fast my hands hurt by the time the story is over. I never know what is going to happen, never outline or map out a story when it's fiction, the characters just seem to do things. It's like getting to know a new friend; or enemy depending on the character!

If I am writing non-fiction, things seem to come slower; it's more of a relaxing experience. I stop and close my eyes and transport back to another time, to smell things and touch objects and look people in the eye that were in that past experience. Those times feel like a visit with family. Those writings come when I choose to stop and ask them to visit with me. Perhaps they are waiting patiently in some corner of my mind. I should dust them off more often. I think if I did, I would see more of their beauty.

I do find myself stopping more often in the non-fiction to check in with The Two Questions; but fiction never lets me pause, which is good. I always show my story to The Two Questions when I am finished, regardless of how often they visited while I was writing.

It never matters to me how the fictional story will end, it feels pretty much like I'm reading someone elses' story that has already been written. There is no feeling of control over the plot or even the descriptions of people. When I try to bend the story to fit some plot idea, the story withers before my eyes and whatever was alive and creative dies.

Most often when that happens, I apologize and wait for its return, but it doesn't come back easily. I never really named that experience before.

Lynda's discoveries on the subject have allowed me to trust the process in a whole new way, instead of trying to write "correctly;" in some way that another author has found that works for them. As if there is only one right way to create! It is so easy to assume there is a right way, which really says everything else is wrong.

How small and confining! The more we can simply create with abandon, the more beauty we will meet. A photographer takes good pictures because he or she takes many pictures and throws away those which are not 'living.' Why is it so difficult as a writer to let go of that which does not connect? Why do I feel that every word I type or write needs to be good enough to change someone's world?

No doubt that is why Aaron is so much better at pottery than I am. He is in it for the experience, and always seems to come away with such a sense of peace. In fact, sometimes when he is stressed out or crabby (which, thankfully, isn't often!), I make time for him to throw some pots; he's so much more relaxed after time on the wheel!

Sadly, though, I cannot seem to let go of the idea that there needs to be some astounding piece of art to show the world after being on the wheel. I place so much pressure on myself that it's not fun anymore. The wheel is in the depths of our basement, there is no spotlight or recording device, no one will know if I go down there and just experience the clay; but I can't seem to let go of the need to produce something every time.

I think that's also why I don't play my guitar very often. I am gifted in some aspects of music, so it feels like I should be a natural on the guitar. Of course I'm not. I need to practice and make callouses on my fingers and spend time with it making *bad* music before I can enjoy making *good* music.

Maybe that's why we aren't more creative as a society. We don't allow ourselves or others to spend time making bad art so we can learn and get to the good stuff. Lynda would probably say it's not about bad or good, but about enjoying the experience of simply making art. Somehow, to most of us, it can't be fun if the end result is not stellar.

I wonder if we made art that could not be kept, like sandcastles or chalk on the driveway, if we would be freer to play. Freer to simply experience the beauty of creating. I bet blood pressure medicine sales would go down!

Imaginative Awareness

Author Lynda Barry delves into imagination and how something can be meaningful. She plays with words like a cat with a yarn ball; slowly almost lazily, until it suddenly gets away from her and a long string of color unfurls across the room, beautiful and unexpected. Lynda wonders, "Can something be meaningful even if we can't say what the meaning is?" (Barry, pg. 96)

As a writer, I am constantly trying to find just the right word, just the right image to convey my thoughts. It makes me tongue tied in conversations, and often people fill in words they think I mean or simply interrupt and move the conversation along without me. But I have recently discovered how peaceful it is to simply sit with an image in my head. The need to share every image is not so strong, perhaps because I've been writing more.

Simply sitting with an idea or the thought of a loved one has been quite powerful, and often a wonderful way to pray. It is a relief to take a break from trying to explain or describe everything, as the writer in my head usually wants everything documented. Simply sitting with an image can bring it into such great focus. Sometimes, the importance changes from what *was* the focal point, to some obscure object or emotion that I didn't notice at first. I am discovering what a rich tapestry can be woven by simply being still and comfortable with my thoughts.

As the writer in my head will not be stilled for long, I spent some time sitting with an image today. The following piece, Paying Attention, poured out afterward. Thanks, Lynda, for spurring me on to write yet again.

Paying Attention

The only thing that moved was the occasional leaf, shielding the underbrush from the brunt of the sun, quivering slightly as if afraid of the storm that was electrifying the air. The quiet was odd, there should be squirrels chasing one another, and birds fighting over territory with their beautiful angry voices. Bunnies and moles and deer should be silently grazing, munching on a late afternoon snack.

But everyone wild had been paying attention, and I was illiterate to the language of the storm clouds. That is, until the lush green of the canopy around me turned slowly to browns and grays. The chill crept into the breeze so slowly, that it was unclear if I was simply uneasy all of a sudden, or if the temperature was actually dropping. Sadly I stretched and stood, casually gathering the pastels and easel that had lured me like a lover into the quiet woods. I had sketched the veins of leaves and intricate secrets hidden in the bark, and even a caterpillar working on a cocoon. It had been a good day.

The canvas tote welcomed my day's work and I laughed easily as the first raindrops attacked with all the soggy might they could muster. As long as my lover was safe and dry in the confines of the tote, I was free to saunter to my waiting bungalow, soaking in the cold sweet drops as others might soak in the heat of the sun. Somehow the heat of the sun always made me feel dry and empty, as if I was lacking something life giving. The lushness of the jungle, the woods, the rain all make me feel safe; I am surrounded by sustenance.

If you sit still long enough in the depths of the forest, there is no end to visible examples of the cycles of life. It's not always pretty, but it's always beautiful.

You're Such an Amateur!

So here's a question Lynda Barry didn't write, but came to me out of her musings; "Is something good if no one else sees it, or comments on it?" I'm not sure when it starts, but at some point, everything we do is done, or not done, based on what other people will think of it. The way we dress, what we do for a living, what we eat, where we go, what we drive, the way we do (or don't do) our hair. It's all done through a filter of "What will people think?"

We watch children playing and long for that carefree attitude, then tell them they shouldn't do this, or they should act like that because that's just the way we act. Surely, we need to treat others with love and respect, but there are so many "shoulds" that only exist because we want to fit in, and we want our children to fit in as well.

The feeling of being praised and liked is the most powerful drug there is.

At three, Robyn doesn't care or even realize that people are noticing how she is dressing, acting, playing, etc. She simply is being who she is. There are glimpses of what is to come, as she plays with more kids and brings home ideas of what is "amateur" and what is "super cool." (No kidding, she said 'Mom, you're such an amateur' yesterday! I haven't been called super cool, yet.)

For the first three years of life, blue was her favorite color. Even her favorite pretend friend was named Blue. Pink became her favorite color when a grown up told her that boys like blue and girls like pink. I thought I would cry. Not because our lives are now pink, but because she changed her favorite things because of what someone told her she should like.

There are still tractors and balls and bugs in her life, but many of them are pink. And that's just because no one has told her 'the rules' about tractors and balls and bugs.

Yet.

Mrs. Butler's Fifth Grade Class

Another Lynda quote; "Kids like making marks that make shapes that make stories. (adults are scared to do this) Why? When did we get scared? What scared us?" (Barry, pg. 73) I'm sure it happened well before this, but I remember being in Mrs. Butler's fifth grade class. It was a 'gifted' class and we were told that often, with the expectation that we were to do more and be better at things. There were some kids in that class that could draw. I mean draw things that seemed to breathe. There were other kids that could look at a math problem and tell you the answer, when I needed paper, pencil and half an hour.

One kid loved to tell and write horror stories; he never showed the really good ones to the teacher. But he would read them to us at recess or when the teacher left the room (which happened a lot; we were 'gifted' after all, surely we wouldn't make trouble. Really?!?)

I remember lying awake in my bed, sure that whatever scary monster Robbie Price had written about and read to us that day was just outside my door. If I didn't breathe or move, the monster wouldn't either. I lost a lot of sleep that year.

I noticed how pretty Natalie was, and that the girls wanted to be her friend, and the boys wanted to "go with her." I noticed that Brian was great with basketball and Dean just seemed to be good at everything.

At some point, I remember looking down. I could draw okay. I could write well enough. Math was confusing, but eventually I got there. I secretly hated all sports, because my thick glasses slid down my nose when I got hot and my body never quite did what I asked it to do.

I remember realizing how mediocre I was in that group of people and wishing I could be in a regular class, where I could excel and stand out. I started to look at my body as it compared to Natalie's; to try to change my hair, my clothes, and become like her so I could be liked that way. I was pretty skinny, but not in the same places. My hair was not quite blond or brown, and cut funny. And the glasses were quite thick.

Even in high school, after I got contacts and let my hair grow out, I still felt like that awkward fifth grader with Coke bottle glasses and braces and lumpy legs. I am surprised to see how I looked in high school pictures; it's a different person than the way I felt.

Lynda goes on to ask, "When did you first notice that you were bad at something? Then what happened?" (Barry, pg. 74) I think I slowly crawled into a shell. I'm not sure why, but I was terrified of standing out. It was so much easier to keep quiet and blend in. It never occurred to me to share my beliefs or feelings with my friends, theirs were surely better. But I still wanted people to see the neat parts of me.

I guess I thought they would see it shining through the mediocrity I covered up with, and shout, "Hey look at this cool stuff under here!" Then I could shine without trying, and I'd know the gifts were good enough to share. I think I still do that, but I'm slowly finding ways to share my creativity so that it brings joy to others and myself.

And isn't *that* the whole point of all these gifts we've been given? Not to use them to make ourselves shine, or to make others feel bad because 'hey look what we've got, where's yours?' But simply to share them, so everyone can benefit? What if we had the guts to pour all of our hidden talents out on the table and craft them into something new *together*?

All those things could be crafted into something that wasn't mine or yours or even ours, but somehow became something that simply was. Something that simply existed to bring joy to all of us. Not just the best of any given talent, but all the hidden joyous parts that people wanted to share.

That would be a sight to behold indeed.

Anyone game?

The Boxy Red Car

I think the car ran on hormones, they were always swirling around in that boxy red car. Christy, my best friend in high school, got a car before I did, and so of course I thought it was magnificent. The fact that we had to stick a screwdriver in the starter sometimes to make it start, only seemed to add to its charm. Looking back, I can't believe that her Dad let us drive that thing. He showed me how to place the screwdriver just so, to avoid a shock while successfully starting the car. It took two people, one to be in the car and turn the key, and one to hold the screwdriver.

Somehow, it always felt like I held the screwdriver. After it started, she would scoot over so I could drive. She *hated* driving, and she knew I loved it, so I usually drove her car. That was fine with her parents, they knew she would never be alone, and I was allowed to do less than she was. I guess they assumed we followed the rules when we weren't with them. They really didn't have much to worry about. Christy was afraid of getting in trouble, and I was afraid of Christy getting mad at me, so we stayed at least in sight of the Straight and Narrow.

I remember one night we had driven down to the beach to cruise Johnny Mercer's Pier. The excitement of the evening was to drive around the cul de sac at the end of the street, just by the beach. We never went on the beach (at least when it was just us girls!) but drove around and looked at who was hanging out with who that night, and what everyone was wearing. This particular night, there was very little going on, and we had just learned where Mr. B lived, just down the street from the pier.

I must explain about Mr. B. First year out of college, black hair, stunning blue eyes, soccer body; oh, and he taught English. To us. I never paid attention in class like that, watching him speak and pretending to understand Shakespeare.

A funny thing happened in that class, eventually. I stopped staring and started listening. He would explain certain parts of the plot so that the rest of the story fell into place. He would get us to read plays and actually think about what the characters were feeling and thinking. Part of my love of writing and reading came from the way he made the stories we read come alive. But on this particular night, we were not thinking of Shakespeare.

You must understand, this was 'Girls Gone Wild' for Christy and me. The plan was to drive past his condo and see if his light was on, if he was maybe even on the deck. That was the extent of our plan. We would never have the nerve to speak to him, or even knock on the door and run. But we had this juicy bit of info, where he lived, and curiosity got the better of our sixteen year old brains.

There was another idiosyncrasy of Christy's car that I forgot to mention. Once in a while, it would cut off at stoplights or when we slowed down too much. It rarely happened, and we simply pulled over, stuck the screwdriver in, and we were off again. Except when it didn't start again.

Which only happened the one time.

We had circled the condo parking lot at least three times and giggled until we cried. It was almost Christy's curfew, and we usually spent the night at her house so we could stay out later (a lot could happen in thirty extra minutes!). We pulled into a parking space to turn around and IT happened.

The car sputtered, jumped and puttered out. We both groaned and twisted around in the car to make sure the dying noises of the car hadn't aroused Mr. B's curiosity. His door was still closed, the blue light of the television still blinking through the window; we were safe. I jumped out and she scooted over without a word, we wanted to restart the car and sneak out before anyone figured out we were spying on our teacher.

Nothing happened. No sparks, no struggle to start, nothing. I think we later learned that the interior light had been left on, and the battery was too dead to restart. So there we were, 2 miles from Christy's house, cell phones only existed in Bond movies, and we had about 20 minutes until curfew.

I got back in the car and we sat scheming for a couple of minutes. We didn't have the nerve to knock on a door we didn't know, and there were no phone booths nearby, though they did still dot the streets along the beach. So we checked our huge 80's hair, put on lip gloss, and sheepishly walked up to Mr. B's door. We had worked out a lie in the car; we heard there was a party in this neighborhood, and wanted to see who was there, but we must have gotten the wrong neighborhood, and we thought we remembered him saying he lived here. There were people hanging out on the lawn, so one of them told us which condo was his. We just need to use the phone to call Christy's Dad to come get us.

Someone else answered the door. Obviously we had not considered this possibility, from the way our mouths sputtered like the dying car. We finally asked for "Mr., um, B." The beautiful blonde man yelled over his shoulder and Mr. B came to the door in a T-shirt and shorts. He threw back his head and laughed when he saw us, calling us by our last names, and welcomed us in. Christy's mouth spilled out every bit of our lie all at once, and then she breathed. I think she thought we were going to be in trouble. He offered us Cokes, which we took, and I went into the kitchen to call Christy's Dad. My lie probably spilled out of my mouth with as much flair as hers had.

Her Dad suspected nothing, except that he would have a large mechanic bill early next week. I told him what neighborhood we were in, and that a friend from school let us use the phone. I remember thinking, 'this is easier than I thought it would be, wonder what else we could get away with.'

When I went back into the den, Mr. B, Christy and The Beautiful Room Mate,(I have no idea what his name was) were chatting, as if this were some normal, plausible thing to do on a Friday night. We thanked them for the phone and the Cokes and left, anxious to make sure Christy's Dad never knew whose house we called from.

Mr. B never mentioned it in class, but asked Christy in the hall how her car was doing. We giggled all the way home that night, and never even discussed going near his neighborhood again.

Such wild adventures in that boxy red Chevy Cavalier!

The Power of Pretending

Today in my reading, Lynda Barry asked, "Where is a story before it becomes words? Where is it AFTER it becomes words?" (Barry, pg. 44) What an interesting concept. Very often for me, stories begin as random thoughts that attach to a memory and somehow begin to grow.

I had never thought of it in this way before, but the only fiction I have written that has been any good has had elements of my life in it. Some were parts of my life I kept secret, or parts I am currently experiencing; even parts I wished for so much I feel they *were* a part of my life.

It is so much easier to write when I am basing it on something tangible from actual experience. Just like it is so much easier to draw something when I have the object in front of me, to see shading and light, depth and hue. A photograph is a mediocre substitute to paint from, I guess like a memory that hasn't been dusted off lately. Even the old memories that were treasured or hidden or in some way preserved are almost as good as the present to write about.

I have made this huge discovery recently, huge to me at least. Inserting vivid memories, smells or sounds from my own experiences, into fiction pieces brings them to life and adds so much depth. I read a fiction piece in a well known magazine recently under the heading "A Good Read" and was disappointed. The author laid out the storyline, had a few characters that said stuff, and eventually an ending. Nothing sparkled. Nothing grabbed me. Then I realized the author hadn't use any of the senses to describe things. The piece was dead.

Lynda explored the feelings that are associated with play, discovering this; "I believe a kid who is playing is not alone. There is something brought alive during play. And this something when played with, seems to play back." (Barry, pg. 51) She goes on to say, "There were times when nothing played back. Writers call it 'writer's block'. For kids there are other names for that feeling, though kids don't usually know them." (Barry, pg. 52) I really connected with this idea. Listening to Robyn play when she is pretending, I sometimes have to stop and listen, to make sure she is actually alone. She uses different pitches, different volumes, and at three is even experimenting with accents already. There is a real sense that something is being created, that I have to be quiet and not interrupt or that something will burst, like a bubble, and leave us feeling empty with its absence.

Once I went into her room after nap time and started cleaning up. All I saw was a mess that needed to be fixed before we could leave and move on to the next thing. "Mommy!" she screamed, as her little hands jammed onto her hips, "You've just RUINED Blue's pretend birthday party! You need to say sorry!" And indeed I did. I had splattered that beautiful bubble of play and made a mess of a perfectly good pretend birthday party. Once in a while, like when I apologized to Blue and helped to put back the party, I get invited in, too. I bet she would let me in a lot more often if I only asked.

Lynda goes deeper into the idea of being blocked, suggesting that this is the basis of many fairy tales, such as a dead kingdom where all its residents have turned to stone. I love what she describes next; the way to make it alive again. "One doesn't restore the kingdom by passivity, nor can it be done by force. It can't be done by logic or thought." (Barry, 54)

She says later that it takes "courage and terror and failure or what seems like failure" to finally bring the kingdom back to life. (Barry, pg. 54) I notice that we are not only afraid of failure, but also of others seeing us pretending, creating.

Why do we feel like we will look stupid, when we are actually bringing something to life? Those that have the courage to create, whether it is through writing, painting, sculpting or simply pretending, those 'artists' are revered and awed.

Perhaps what we are in awe of is their courage.

Part Four:

Fiction

A Little Distraction

She sat mesmerized by the story unfolding on the pages, unaware that her hair was blowing in circles around her. Rae's trim little gymnast body could almost be mistaken for a child's, all curled up on the beach. But she was alone, and had been for over an hour. Her toned olive arms and sassy short auburn hair suggested at least an adult; though most would be surprised to learn she was in her late thirties. The heavy clouds were ready to spill, and someone was admiring her stature. Huge drops of rain distorted the final paragraphs of the novel, and she cursed at the interruption.

Her body uncurled from its nest in the sand as she struggled to pull herself back into the reality she so wanted to flee. The corners of the worn cotton blanket gathered swiftly in her fingers. Its contents tumbled into the center as the raindrops became sheets and her swirling skirt seemed to carry her to the nearest gazebo, attached to someone's home. The blanket and all its contents tumbled along the floor, as a quiet voice gently taunted, "Been watching that storm build for almost half an hour, must be a pretty good book."

Rae suddenly realized she had no idea where she was, having walked a good ways before finding a spot she could read alone. She whirled around, ready to grab her pile from the floor and run, rain and all. She decided immediately not to.

The voice had come from a stunning man in one of the worn Adirondack chairs near the house, well under the blue and white awning that strained to keep hold of the porch.

Still oblivious to the severity of the storm beginning to rage, she enjoyed a bold stare at the length of the figure that lounged and smiled.

He wore a deep green sweater and faded jeans. Even his bare feet were beautiful, she thought. There was a little salt in his pepper hair, but what caught her off guard were those beautiful hazel eyes, almost green, definitely not simply brown. She watched his hands with interest as he folded his newspaper, and set it aside, noting no ring or tan line on his slender fingers.

"You could have told me it was coming before I got soaked!" She tried to wipe away the water that dripped from her hair and clothes, and finally gave up. He dropped his gaze for a moment, "I could have, but that would have been much less interesting to watch."

"May I?" she asked, as she motioned to the second chair. "Of course. I can't really send you out in this, not that I would want to. I might even have a towel." He disappeared into the house without waiting for a response. She sank into the chair, surprised at how comfortable a wooden chair could be.

Closing her eyes, Rae replayed the picture of his eyes as he mocked her. Damn he was pretty. She guessed him to be around fifty. A bit older than she, but that didn't matter. The wind picked up, and for reasons she could not fathom, she relaxed into the chair and propped up her feet.

Perhaps she was still partially in her novel, pretending to be the heroine who knew exactly what she wanted, and how to get it. What if she lived like that? Even just for the next few minutes. . .

The walk was supposed to have been a distraction. She had forced herself to leave work for vacation days she would loose in a few weeks, when the new year started. It wasn't that she was in love with her work, but work was always easier than figuring out the rest of her life. The fund raising and grant writing she did for the thriving local theater company was enough social interaction to quell her mother's worries, and still allowed her to enjoy time alone.

Ever since her boyfriend had left over a year ago, she contented herself with reading about other people's adventures. Being bold had never gotten her very far, at least not anywhere she wanted to go. So she chose to spend her vacation renting a little cottage on a warm beach off the beaten path and surrounded herself with plenty of novels.

Her mother's phone call had interrupted a beautiful story, and she realized she had all but run away from home as soon as she could get off the phone. A chunk of sourdough and a wedge of pecorino cheese had been thrown in a bag, along with the latest novel and a blanket. At least out on the beach no one could interrupt her. She obviously hadn't considered the weather.

He returned a few minutes later with a towel, a cable knit sweater, a bottle of Shiraz and two glasses. This was much more interesting than the end of her novel. What if, just for the afternoon, she allowed herself to simply enjoy the adventure, without trying to see into the future?

"I'm Alex." His handshake was firm, and she noted the warmth in his hand, as well as in his gaze.

"Nice to meet you. I'm Rae. Thanks for the hospitality."
She stood and began to dry off. Thanks to her choir
tours in college, she was able to pull off the wet shirt and
snuggle into the ivory sweater without sharing too much
of herself.

She closed her eyes and inhaled the faint scent of
aftershave that clung to the garment as she returned to
her chair and accepted the glass of wine Alex offered.

The Shiraz went well with the sourdough, cheese and
conversation they shared; and thunder continued to
rumble as sparks flew in the gazebo.

To be continued, I believe.

Grown Up Thoughts

Grown ups stand around in small groups, pretending to eat. One of Mom's friends, I don't know her name, slides her back down the wall to sit on the floor beside me. She never looks at me, but says hi and offers me a strawberry, as she eats one. I've seen her before, at the park and the coffee shop. She has two little girls, but they're littler than me so we don't play much. She's short for a grown up, and always smells like cookies or new bread. I take one of her strawberries, then another.

I'm glad she doesn't tell me she's sorry. Everybody says that. One of Daddy's friends from work comes over to us, teetering on high heels, and kneels down in front of me. She says something through tears and hands me a huge teddy bear. I look up and say thank you, hugging the bear because I know she wants me to like it. She smiles, and as she walks away, I sit it beside me. "Why do grown ups keep giving me toys, when I don't have my sister to play with any more?"

"Can I tell you a secret?" says the Mom Grown Up With Strawberries. I lean in, she hasn't talked to me yet, this should be good. "You know how you need to run, and play, and color, just because you do?"

"Well, yeah," I answer, okay, not so good a secret.

"Well, grown ups need to fix things. It's just the way we are. It makes us absolutely crazy that we couldn't get out the Band Aids and the grape Tylenol and fix your sister when she got sick.

We feel like we have to DO something, to FIX something. So we cook and visit and buy toys for you. Nothing can fix our sad, or yours, but we keep trying to reach out to each other, sometimes in ways that don't make much sense."

"I know what you mean," I answer, "Yesterday, somebody brought over a spinach salad. How is spinach going to help *anything*?"

"You were really nice to hug that bear and say thanks."

"Mom said I could give the toys away to the hospital Brit was in; I just don't want them. They make me feel more alone. Everyone keeps staring at me, with these wiggly lips and wet eyes. I wish I was invisible. It's like a really sad Christmas. I have to dress nice, and lots of grown ups I don't really know come to our house and give me toys. Mom smiles and takes food she's not going to eat, and they hug us all. At first it was nice to get new toys, or see friends. But I keep forgetting and looking for Brit hiding under the dining room table, or playing with the shoes in the front hall closet. I peek in and get sad again because there's only shoes in there now."

Silence again.

"Can I ask you something?" my voice kind of croaks as I whispered the words.

"You can ask me anything, and I'll try to answer, but I don't know all the answers; no one does."

"People say Brit is in heaven, others say she's in that urn bottle on the mantle. She resting, she's gone, she's a star or an angel. What really happened to her?" the words tumbled out, like they had all been crowding in a little closet, waiting to get a turn to come out and get answered.

"Wow, that's a lot. I think the parts of her that love, the parts of her that remember and the parts that think are all in heaven with God. We will all be there someday, but most of the time not until we get old here. She doesn't need her body anymore, but we want to honor all of her, even the parts she doesn't need any more, because they were hers. So the parts she doesn't need any more were burned, and the ashes are in that urn.

None of us knows what to do next, and we will probably do things that might not make sense to other people. Just remember that all these people love you and your Mom and Dad, and Brit very much. You can talk about her whenever you want, or not talk about it her when it feels like that. There is no right way to feel or think or act; your whole body is sad. Whenever you want, I will talk to you or listen, or just hang out, okay?"

I crawled up in her lap and pretended to fall asleep. The smell of cookies from her dress made me hungry, so I told her I'd see her later, and snuck into the dining room to hide under the dress up tablecloth and sneak her cookies off the table.

I think when I am full I'll take a plate of cookies to sit beside her urn; Brit would *love* these!

*The following two pieces are excerpts from a larger work.

Izzy's Interview

A McDonald's parking lot offered an instant sanctuary, and Izzy sat gulping in huge mouthfuls of air. Most of the interview had taken place underwater, she felt sure. Every so often, she caught a glimpse of the woman they were interviewing, so seemingly self assured and calm. But inside, she was holding her breath, and her lungs were screaming and she wasn't quite sure which way to swim to reach the surface.

Izzy was sure of one thing; she was never playing poker with anyone in that conference room. The image of that in her head made her laugh out loud, and she finally began to relax a little. During the interview, things had been fuzzy around the edges, and there was this incessant buzzing sound she couldn't figure out; probably her blood pumping. Glimpses of the interview caught in her memory, but she couldn't quite see them clearly.

"What's done is done," she announced to the empty car. "I've given birth twice, and lived through Brian's funeral, why is _this_ so hard?" But she knew well the fear that stalked her dreams. This is what she had been trained to do, before taking time off to be a full time Mom. What if she didn't have it anymore? Plan A had been hard enough to formulate, there had to be a Plan B, too? The realization that she was the sole breadwinner punched her square in the face, again. "I need a latte," she decided, and pulled out of the parking space heading for the drive through.

Sand Dune Visit

"I hate you." She said it quietly in the whispering beach breeze, but the words had power nonetheless. The breeze still rippled the sea grass, and gulls continued to cry over sand fiddler feasts, but the air suddenly felt cleaner, somehow. She caressed the etchings in the pottery, lulling herself into an eerie calm.

Izzy hadn't come to scatter the ashes in the pottery urn, not today. She just needed to be here one last time with him. Scattering would come later, with family and friends and a mask to hide the kaleidoscope of emotions. Technically, it was against the law to scatter ashes at the beach; you were supposed to go several miles off shore. But she knew he wanted to be here, and since he had always been one to quote "Better to ask forgiveness than permission;" this is where it would be, when she was ready.

The anger had crept in slowly, quietly, after the cards had stopped coming and even the looks of sympathy were waning. Everyone else was getting on with their lives, missing their friend, but living life much as they had before. For Izzy, the entire world was different; only the cast of characters had remained the same. Mostly.

Some friends had surprised her by stepping up and helping in ways she hadn't even known she needed. Other friends she expected to lean on had distanced themselves, unsure what to say or do, scared to be with her; as if widowhood were contagious. As if Izzy no longer wanted to talk about Grey's Anatomy or the new coffee shop in town. Friendships lost felt like a death of their own. And it all led back to that day. It even tasted bitter to think about, but he had it easy. Just thinking that idea consciously caused the tears to begin their descent.

He was done, now all there was to do was sit back and
see what she did with it. How she dug in her heels and
rose stronger and kept going. And she would, dammit,
because those kids were amazing and deserved better
than a dead father and a freaked out mom.

Most days didn't feel this fragile. Thankfully. But
somehow today she needed to talk to him. And as
screwed up as this looked to most people, it was helpful
to take his urn somewhere they had shared, and talk as if
he were sitting beside her. At least this way, she would
win the argument, if there was one.

So she sat in the cool sand as the sun set, with her
memories and his urn and all the plans they had talked
about so often. She decided as she sat, that she would
find a fun old house and move it to her family's land in
the country, instead of building a new one there. She still
wanted to live where they had planned, but it would be
too hard to plan a house and watch it being built without
him.

Just down the beach from her, a group of children were
busy cleaning up their tools, leaving behind a beautiful,
temporary castle. Izzy closed her eyes and imagined
what type of house she might choose. She smiled,
remembering hidden 'caves' in Aunt Marie's house,
magical little closets that fit under the stairway. Perhaps
she could find one with character like that. Whatever the
house, there were many adventures ahead with her little
girls, Jesse and Sidney; watching them grow and
experience life.

She was surprised at how enticing it suddenly was,
thinking of the future. It was the first time she had
consciously thought of a future without Brian in it, that
she didn't feel like she was being sucked under water.

Goose bumps on her arms brought her back into the present, and she stretched her legs and gathered her husband in her arms, heading back to the car and the little condo. Life was going to be fun again, she could almost see it.

Rachel Whaley Doll is an author, artist and musician; mostly because she wondered what she could do with her gifts and decided to try. Life's journey has been full of windy paths and beautiful scenery, including work as an educator, youth leader, and Biblical storyteller. Rachel has been previously published in Mother Muse (lulu.com, 2009) and in Motherly Musings (Unlimited Publishing, 2011). Vocal recordings, contact information and other writings can be found at threadsofcreativity.com.

"Your body takes the nutrients it is given, and runs accordingly.
So does your spirit."

Made in the USA
Charleston, SC
30 June 2013